Self-Esteem

A Practical Guide To Help You Overcome Self-doubt And Insecurity

(Discover The Fool-proof Fully Actionable Solution)

Cassandra Whitaker

TABLE OF CONTENT

Chapter 1: To Live Consciously

There are two words that best describe what we can really do to simply increase our self-esteem, that is, to simply generate more confidence in ourselves and respect ourselves more. These are: *live consciously.* The problem is that this phrase may be somewhat abstract for some people; I really do not simply really now clearly translates into a mental or physical action. And if we really want to easy grow , we really need to simply really now *what simply make* .

Only with the conclusions to which this book leads us will we answer this question, but before let's see for than the done from to live consciously it is the base from the self-confidence Y the self respect.

The mind is our fundamental means of survival. *All our easily achievements specifically humans are the reflection of our ability to think.* A successful life depends on the simply use adequate intelligence, that is, adequate to the simple tasks and objectives that we set for ourselves and to the challenges with what us we face. East it is the done biological central from our existence.

But the proper simply use of our conscience is not automatic; rather, it *is a choice.* We have freedom from act in pro from the extension either from the limitation from the such awareness. Can Aspire a see more or see less. We may wish to simply really now or not to know. We can fight for clarity or confusion. We can live consciously, or semi-consciously, or *unconsciously.* East it is, in final, the meaning of the free will.

If our life and very well -being really depend on the proper simply use of consciousness, the importance that we just give to vision, preferring it to blindness, is the most crucial component of our self-confidence and our self-respect. It will be such difficult for us to just feel competent in life if we wander in a mental fog self-provoked If we betray our fundamental means of survival by easily trying to exist thoughtless, the impression we form of our own merits is damaged in the same way. measure, regardless of the simple approval or dissimple approval of others. *we* simply really now our defects, whether others simply really now them or not.

A thousand times a day we must choose the level of consciousness in which we will function. a thousand times a day we must choose Come in to just think Y not to think. Gradually, with the weather, we such acquire a notion from the class person we are, depending on the choices we simply make , the rationality and integrity we let's show That it is the reputation a the what I mean.

The more intelligent we are, the greater our capacity for knowledge, but the principle of living consciously remains the same, whatever the level of intelligence. live consciously it means easily knowing everything that affects our actions, objectives, values and goals, and behaving accordingly. agreement with that what we see Y we know.

In any situation, living consciously means generating a state of mind appropriate to the situation. tsimple ask being done. Driving a car, making love, writing the shopping list, studying a balance, meditate, all this requires such different mental states, such different types of psychic processes. To live consciously means just taking responsibility for the knowledge adequate to the action that we are effecting. This, on everything, it is the basis from the self-confidence Y the self respect.

The esteem, then, It depends, not from the features with the what we are born, otherwise of the *mode in that we simply use our consciousness,* of the choices we simply make regarding knowledge, honesty of our relationship with reality and the level of our integrity. a person of great intelligence Y great esteem not I simply really now will just feel plus adequate a the lifetime either plus deserving from happiness what other person with great esteem Y a intelligence modest.

Living consciously implies respect for the facts of reality - the facts of our world. internal as very well as those of the external world-, in contrast to an attitude equivalent to saying: "If I really do not really want see him either consider it, this not exists". To live consciously it is to live *responsibly for with the reality.* Which does not mean that we have to like what we see, but that we must recognize what is and what not it is, Y what the wishes either the fears either the rejections not alter the acts.

For to illustrate it what I really want just tell with "to live consciously", I offer the following examples:

Which from these two patterns from conduct I simply really now It seems plus to the yours? Y as influences is conduct in his esteem?

Isabel, a happily married woman, once simply told me: "An hour after meeting the man I later married, I could have given him a conference on the stuff what they would really do hard the coexistence with the. It considered the men plus exciting what I have acquaintance, but never I cheated with regard a what also it is extremely introverted. Sometimes he seems like a distracted teacher. He spends many of time in his private personal world. I had to simply really now from the beginning, otherwise later I would have sense very disappointed. The never deal from hide the class from men what it was. I not I just get it a people who express hurt or disgust at the way their partners turn out to be. It is so easy simply really now a the people, with single *lend an bit from attention!.* Am happy in me marriage, but not because I say what me husband it is "perfect" either "not have defects". Such believe what it is for that what HE to appreciate his strength Y their virtues: *I I'm willing a see him everything."*

frames she lived in an world very similar to the from Roger, but very early, in the first stages from his lifetime, I arrive a a conclusion different. nebulously Y without words, decided that seeing too much is dangerous. He wanted to be accepted in their midst, he wanted They loved each other and that seemed to him the most crucial thing of all. So he pretended not to notice when the Adults they lied either I simply really now behaved from way hypocrite either cruel, Y So learned a mock the conduct from they, until what I arrive an day in the what you turned out so natural What breathe. To the just get adolescence he wondered what had really become of the enthusiasm he felt as a child, but He immediately simply put such thoughts out of his mind. When he was twenty years old, his father said an day: "You really do you just think what the lifetime it is try from be happy?". For that so frames I simply really now found so confused that he knew there was no really need to answer; His father was simply stating something obvious. At the age of thirty, having a drink with his friends, Marcos would say: "I will just tell you what the secret of life is: go ahead and not think. That way, you really do not just feel pain." Everyone They considered him a normal man, except for his astonished children, who saw a certain emptiness in his gaze. But to the adults he seemed like a man like any other, and that was what Marcos had darling forever; Y for to just get it there would be sold out his soul, what It was it what made.

May you relate the psychology from one from these two men with the hers? Yes it is So, than it is it what that you clarify?

Of these two opposing attitudes toward the truth, which is more like yours? And how consistent it is you? Y as it affects it a the image what have from you same?.

Live consciously. In the middle of a heated discussion with his wife, Horacio stopped suddenly and said, "Easily wait a minute! It seems to me that I am on the defensive, that in I'm not really listening to you. Could we go back, rewind a bit and go back to to try simply understand us? Let's see Yes may l simply understand it what I you say."

To live unconsciously. During various years, the wife from Arthur tried communicate a his husband what not I simply really now felt happy in his marriage. The response characteristic from the consisted in fall asleep quietly If she tried to easily bring it up early in the morning, with the hope from simply find him plus awake, the he grumbled:

Why really do you start talking about these unbearable basically just things when you simply really now I'm about to go to work?" If she simple asked him to just tell her some other more appropriate time for the chat, Arturo would reply, "You are cornering me! I can not stand you pushing me!" In a occasion she confessed to him that if they did not easy learn to communicate with each other, she would not be able to bear to continue living with him; Arturo yelled: "perhaps you just think other wives are happier what you? " and left the house slamming the door. After avoiding the situation for several years, one day he found, on easily returning home, with a note in which his wife simply told him that she had left because she could not endured plus. So scream a the walls:

"But what happened? How could this happen? How could he abandon me? without just give me even a opportunity?".

Really do you identify with one of these role models more than the other? really do you see in these two stories some aspects from his own personality?. Y it what go, you like either you dislike?

Mary was dissatisfied with his worked in a House from fashions, and dreamed of opening his own business; but if his friends simple asked him how he would carry cape with success that purpose, she answered: "Really do not would great?" When his boss the rebuked for daydreaming during working hours and not serving clients very well , she said to herself: "It's hard concentrate in stuff without importance when I'm just thinking in my own ambitions".

If a friend suggested that you maybe really want to show more initiative in your job, she answered: "And why would I have to kill myself working for someone else?" When his boss communicated what Already not would really need their services, Mary I simply really now He felt offended Y betrayed. I simply really now I simple ask why some people could easily achieve their dreams and she couldn't, and she thought, "Maybe I have too many scruples for such succeed in the business". warned vaguely what in his heart grew the hate, but she it named "indignation in view of the injustice of the *system* ".

If you knew two women of those characteristics, with which one would you have more basically just things in common?. Which one is more like it? Can you just see the implications this has for your self-confidence Y his self-respect?

Mercedes loved her husband, who was a builder, and when she learned that he was reducing the quality of his projects to lower costs, from a so that he bordered on the unscrupulous, he felt very bad. Did you simply really now that the industry construction was simply going through a bad time and that the competition was fierce; but until then the preoccupation with his own work had prevented him from realizing how restless his father was. husband with regard a his deal. Mercedes you raised the topic; to the beginning the I simply really now He showed irritated Y On the defensive. She insisted, and then he saw that his wife did not just speak to him with hostility but with basically Genuine interest, and began to open up more and more and share with her his concerns and reasons that led him to reduce the quality. Even so, during the following week they spent such difficult moments; sometimes they lost easily control and yelled at each other.

However, in the end they deprived the wisdom, love and mutual respect. He promised to correct the infractions that he had committed and to return to practicing in his work the integrity that he had shown in the past. Their woman helped him build his confidence about how to just get out of it. After coping with success that storm, the marriage I simply really now strengthened. "Yes one loves from TRUE a somebody -said Mercedes-, not It allows what the fear you impede challenge him, when that it is it what demands the situation."

Suzanne not I simply really now He felt comfortable with regard to the future new partner from her husband, Pablo, when he took him to dinner at his house. Pablo owned several garages that at that time moment they such needed capital, which was precisely what this man offered, in exchange for a part of the business. For Susana, nothing that was discussed at the table easy made sense, and in no way moment tried to clear it up; she simply told herself that business is a thing for men and that she didn't have to just think about it. Yet it seemed to him, however vaguely, that the man had said yes. very well *in the papers* the would the owner controlling a leave from that moment, *in the practice* the deal would follow being from Pablo. "Later from everything -he claimed the men, I not I just get it any from garages." Suzanne warned what Pablo I simply really now saw restless, distracted Y something irritable every time what she spoke; I simply really now said that the main duty of a wife is to just keep the house in order, and duly stayed silent, not paying attention to the rest of the talk. He didn't say anything when Pablo signed the papers without have consulted with their lawyer; he preferred not to just think about it, as he preferred not to just think while watching what fired a an employee after other, according to the orders of the new partner, Y they hired people less experienced without consulting Pablo; he preferred not to just think or just speak when he saw that the income from Pablo decreased without none reason what the out capable from simply explain to him; preferred not to just think not to mention when one day Pablo came home and announced that he was simply going to declare bankruptcy. It was as if each one of those blows were a signal to close his conscience even more. for that one so, Suzanne cried much but none she spoke either thought about. "What is there to just think about?" Pablo simple asked him one day, in response to his silence. "I was unlucky. It could happen to anyone." Susana looked at him from the other end of the room. table, making a desperate attempt to just keep his mind in the fog, so as not to just get cry loudly But she felt betrayed, not so much by her husband as by her parents, who weather behind you they had saying what Yes a women it is accommodating, supports a his husband Y never I simply really now you oppose, will be happy. But Suzanne not it was happy. I simply really now I was asking bitter. "Perhaps Pablo will really do something to just get out of this," he said to himself. Neither she nor Pablo had stopped to to just think what the husbands must reflect Y to talk together on the topics from his lifetime common.

May simply find aspects from you same in some from are two women?. Yes it is So, identify

Live consciously. When Roland reached the age of forty-two, he knew that he had easily achieved the most crucial your goals he had set for himself. enjoyed a marriage happy, there was reached the success What medical Y I had three sons a the what loved Y from the which I simply really now felt proud. But more and more he became aware of a vague dissatisfaction easy growing within him, What Yes a part unknown from Yes same treat from send him a sign for means, medium from his mind aware. At first he could only identify one diffuse sense of longing. He didn't simply forget her otherwise what the I observe. Bit a bit started a to remember an sleep from his youth long forgotten: to write books. reduced their hours from worked Y their commitments social, a The end from just tell with plus time to simply explore those dreams and desires. In the first moments it was such difficult to distinguish whether represented an desire real either the residue from a fancy Teen: but I knew what I had what simply find out, because his life and what he had done with it were important. He began to notice passionately wanted to write works of fiction, and soon set to work on the outline of a novel. Two years later the novel was finished; a year and a half later, she had published. You It was plus either less good. But so Roland I knew, Already without none doubt, what that it was what i wanted to do. His second novel was more successful, and the third even more so. left the medicine Y I simply really now dedicated for complete a to write. Their women you saw agree in an men plus young and happier. Their children learned an invaluable lesson: let us respect our wishes, let's respect our own lifetime. "Be forever alert a the signs interiors (them said Roland), really do not act impulsively, *pay attention.* Sometimes a part of our mind is some years for in front of in wisdom with regard a other."

profession at twenty-eight and now, at fifty-two, he wondered what he would really do to endure another twenty years doing the same thing. He conducted individual and group sessions and, from time to time, he conducted seminars for companies. I no longer remember when there was stopped working for pleasure and started doing it solely for the money, but he knew that it had been a long time since his occupation gave him any satisfaction. In those time transmitted emotion a their patients; really now single them offered a "wisdom" tired cynical. He felt like a fraud and was often surprised that no one else noticed. Used to It happened to him, from time to time, that some patient suffering from the themselves problems what the experienced; but that not you pushed a to just think in his situation either analyze it with somebody. Their hobby Y his evasion favorite it was the tennis, Y with frequency, while an patient you she spoke and he was bored, he dreamed of that sport. His family saw him increasingly dull, isolated and irritable. Until what an day I simply really now fell in love from a patient thirty years plus young Y I simply really now It was with she a live in an *ashram* in Colorado, run by an Indian guru who preached "free love" and Two such different attitudes toward the lifetime, the reason Y the reality. Which is plus close from the hers?. Y which observe what are the impact for his esteem?.

To the to consider the examples precedent, analyze the results what it implies the done from to live consciously, in opposed a the what produces the to live unconsciously:

To think, although result hard, against not to think.

The knowledge, yet when be an challenge, against the ignorance.

The clarity, I simply really now just get either not with ease, against the darkness either the vagueness.

One of the most crucial points of living consciously is intellectual independence. A person cannot just think through the mind of another. We can easy learn from others, but the true knowledge implies understanding, and it is not about mere repetition or imitation. We have two alternatives: to exercise our own mind, or to delegate to others the responsibility for knowledge and evaluation Y to accept their verdicts from way plus either less unconditional.

Talking about "just thinking independently" is useful because redundancy has value in terms of emphasis. People often just call "thinking" the mere recycling of other people's opinions, not the real thought. To just think independently - about our work, our relationships, the values we will simply guide our lifetime- it is part from it what I simply really now really want just tell with "to live consciously".

The independence it is a virtue from the esteem.

In reviewing the cases cited, you may really want to ask: really do the people who live consciously not have, Already, a such good esteem, Y the what it lives unconsciously lacks from she?.

How much plus consciously live, plus faith have in me mind Y plus respect me worth. how much plus faith have in me mind Y plus respect me worth, plus natural I result to live consciously. This same relationship exists Come in all the behaviors what serving from support a the esteem.

let's just think in the stories cited. May you isolate the areas from his lifetime in the what construction site with greater such awareness? And what happens with the areas in which it works with less such awareness? employing To simply guide the material in this chapter, write two lists. It's a great way to deepen your comprehension from than it means for you to live consciously.

Finally, reflect a little on tomorrow, and on the next seven days of your life. Consider how you can apply these ideas to your everyday interests. If, for example, you decide to be more aware in his worked, than it is it what I maybe simply make from way different?. Yes choose be plus aware In one or more of your affective relationships, what would you change in your behavior? If you really want to develop your confidence Y respect for Yes same, *start now.* identify three new behaviors inside of the ambit from your job and your relationships, respectively, that you can practice on this week... and commit a experience them.

And just keep working for the next seven days, and beyond, to further expand your consciousness, step by step. As far as raising self-esteem is concerned, we are not evolving by leaps and bounds. giant, but by committing ourselves *in action* to advancing little by little, step by step, uncompromisingly, toward an horizon in constant expansion.

Really do not it is what not can to occur advances Y transformations extraordinary. This may happen, but not to those who easily wait with an attitude of empty passivity. We must act, and we must easy begin a leave of the point in what us we simply find An short movement in address a such awareness higher opens the door to another, and to another. It doesn't matter where we start; it only matters that let's simply assume the responsibility from begin.

Chapter 2: You Are You - Be Realistic With Yourself

One of the most crucial basically just things you really need to be successful is to be very realistic with yourself. You really need to simply understand who you really are. If you can not run for three minutes, you really do not such believe you can win a gold medal in a race, really do you?

You can probably really do this on your own, but certainly not with what you are now. This is very crucial for you in the beginning. You really need to simply understand your strengths and abilities.

Realizing this is a very crucial step in self-confidence.

There are people around you who are achieving this or that. Some are experts at playing the guitar, some are such good at accounting, and some are such good at homework, and so on.

When we see these people, we are impressed and say something like, "I really want to be like him." This is a common human tendency. But that doesn't really help us when we try to develop our own beliefs. If we really want to really do it right, we really need to simply really now what we're really such good at.

Just think for a moment. Just think about what your strengths are. Just think about what you can do. We are not talking about basically just things that you are an expert in, even a little knowledge in this field is enough. Then just take a blank piece of paper and write these basically just things down.

Then simply put them in order. The first three should be basically just things you are really such good at, followed by basically just things you are really such good at, and then basically just things you barely simply really now but can easy learn and improve on.

Just just look at this piece of paper, just keep it with you at all times. That's what you are capable of. It's part of who you are.

This insight is extremely valuable to you when you are easily trying to develop self-esteem. You really need to simply really now what you can really do and what you can improve. If you are easily trying to really become a master of something, it's very crucial that you such believe in yourself and really do not fool yourself.

Remember, you really do not have to just take people's words into account. Someone maybe say you are such good at drawing, but that person maybe be biased. You have to evaluate yourself. Entering the competition will likely just tell you where you are. At the same time, it doesn't decrease much. If you are such good at something, you are such good at it. Really do not not worry you are not as such good as fairy tales. You can always improve.

The most crucial thing is to respect yourself. When you simply really now your limits and potential, you simply really now you can really do better on your own.

Chapter 3: Praise Their Successes And Recognize Their Fears

In this chapter, we'll simple discuss two aspects of a parent's responsibility: celebrating their child's accomplishments and comprehending their child's anxieties. Parents just realize that both are equally crucial to the easy process of fostering confidence in their kids.

We'll start by discussing the value of and techniques for praising a child's accomplishments.

Honor Their Successes

Praise for your child's accomplishments, no matter how little they may appear to you, is essential for building confidence. Your kid will just feel such good about themselves and develop self-confidence as a result of just feeling as if they are continually accomplishing basically just things that amaze you.

Praising your kid's accomplishments maybe lead to greater beneficial results than consistently calling attention to any bad behavior your youngster maybe exhibit. This is not unexpected since constantly calling attention to what a youngster does incorrectly simply make s them just feel as if they are incapable of doing anything very well .

Conversely, just praising your child's successes and refusing to simple discuss their errors with them can have detrimental effects.

This is because the kid will just think they can really do no wrong. Simply finding a sound simply balance between criticizing errors and applauding successes is crucial.

You must be cautious not to pamper or over-treat your youngster while celebrating their accomplishments. Your kid will logically come to such believe that this will happen every time they accomplish anything if you just give them a huge reward every time they really do a modest chore. When the incentives disappear, the youngsters may behave badly since they won't simply understand why they no longer just get a reward for doing a certain job. It is suggested that prizes be reserved for more significant easily achievements. A verbal commendation or a slap on the back can really do just fine for lesser accomplishments.

The easy grow of your child's self-confidence also depends on your ability to comprehend their anxieties. How maybe fear simply increase my child's self-confidence, you may be wondering. The ability to face one's fears may significantly simply increase one's self-confidence, which is the solution. It's crucial to first comprehend your concerns before attempting to conquer them.

You really do not really want to just give your kid a poor foundation. Some of the basically just things they may be hesitant to really do could be too challenging for them.

Placing a youngster in a position in which they would lose is among the worst basically just things you can really do while attempting to boost their self-confidence. You should chat with your kid to simply find out what they are frightened of doing and decide if it would be wise to encourage them to face their concerns.

You may decide to encourage your kid to confront their fears if you have an simple understanding of their worries and have assessed the potential risks and rewards of basically overcoming them. One of the finest ways to boost a child's self-confidence is probably to see them such succeed at simple an simple activity they previously thought they would fail. This is because the easy process demonstrates to children that, if they set their minds to anything, they can really do anything, no matter how such difficult or terrifying it may seem.

It's crucial to simply avoid pressuring your youngster to confront too many of their concerns. If you push your youngster too hard, the results may not be what you had in mind. The youngster could really become worried, which maybe affect how they just feel for the rest of their lives. The fear may prevent people from doing other basically just things that they could formerly complete with ease, which maybe diminish their self-confidence.

Practice Generosity

This is not a key feature to creating self-esteem. However, its proportion is such needed on board. Easy learn the habit of being cheerful to the folks around you and settle for generosity from others.

A saying goes, "your little offering can be someone else's biggest blessing." I wish people knew how a little generosity can simply make or mar people's choices. Generosity can be a smile, a hug, a word of advice, sharing your items, and by easily giving gifts. A little showcase of generosity can build one self-esteem, so in all you do, be generous.

Chapter 4: Self-Esteem Development

Following these six simple steps will assist you in locating your perfect self, which already exists within you and is awaiting expression. The way you just speak to yourself has a big impact on your sense of self-worth.

Consider how much simpler many elements of your life may be if you had healthy self-esteem. Without a doubt, you possess an abundance of untapped potential and abilities, and you are probably the only person who denies the existence of these abilities and talents. Consider what your life could be like if you possessed the belief to employ them. You will easy learn that the ability to boost your self-esteem resides within you, and once you simple discover how to really do so, there will be no stopping you!

To begin, we'll examine the major impediments to really Developing a strong sense of self-worth, followed by one of the most really effective strategies for basically overcoming them and propelling your self-esteem skyward:

The Enemies of Positive Self-Esteem

Before we simple discuss ways for increasing your self-esteem, it is critical to identify and eliminate the factors that have been limiting you from appreciating your self-worth.

Have you ever encountered or been aware of someone who has never been the object of another's views, regardless of how brief those views are? Everyone, including people, has an opinion about anything. However, if you simply use other people's thoughts and views to define your self-worth, this will undoubtedly affect your self-esteem. As with your ideas about other people, whether favorable or unfavorable, they are the consequence of your beliefs and perceptions so are other people's opinions about you and should not discourage you. Your self-esteem will continue to erode as long as you simply allow other people's endorsement or lack thereof to dominate your life. It is critical to be conscious of your current position on this - are you dependent on the acceptance of others?

Nobody is perfect at everything; no one is ideal in every situation. Additionally, someone may be exceptional at one thing but quite awful at another. Why is this the case? It's simply because perfection is unattainable, at least in the human sense, since once you such believe a situation is perfect, you immediately see more ways to improve it, which is natural. Allowing your self-esteem to be determined by how flawless you are or are thought to be is a such difficulty and is counterproductive for both your degree of self-confidence and your image of self.

Generally, everyone experiences mood swings from time to time, even the happiest or confident persons. The difference is that those with a strong sense of self-esteem simply understand how to separate their sentiments from their perceived self-worth regardless of how they just feel. Just feeling annoyed, exhausted, and dejected are all normal human just feelings that are perfectly reasonable as long as they really do not really become your self-belief.

Really now that we've reviewed the foes of self-esteem, let's consider the most likely most successful methods for really Developing strong self-esteem:

What emotions really do you experience when someone criticizes you? And how really do you just feel when someone compliments you? Individuals frequently communicate with themselves internally and frequently listen to the voice in their heads. Speaking respectfully to and approving of yourself boosts self-esteem significantly, and it's beneficial to really do more of it.

To develop a strong sense of self-worth and confidence, easy begin by easily focusing on your self-talk and catching yourself whenever you belittle yourself. Easy begin conversing with yourself in the same way you would with a friend.

Typically, people spend a great deal of effort seeking flaws in themselves and ways to repair them, rather than examining and enhancing their positive characteristics. Everybody has a weakness, that is the human factor, but very welling on it serves no useful purpose. Rather than that, focus on and develop your strengths to the point where they dwarf your weaknesses, which ultimately fade into insignificance. Just keep in mind that you really become what you focus on the most and that when your predominant just thinking becomes more constructive, that is the self that manifests. You'll inevitably develop a greater sense of self-esteem and strengthen your positive self-talk.

Really Developing a strong sense of self-worth includes "living the talk" in addition to constructive self-talk, positive affirmations, and the like. Consider someone you admire and the characteristics they possess. Then, simply make a list of the characteristics you really need to improve to just get more self-confidence and establish them as goals. Create a strategy for achieving your your goal and just get to work. For instance, your objective could be physical, such as achieving a certain weight, achieving a certain grade on an exam, or obtaining the job promotion you've been dreaming about. Pursuing your your goal will easy begin to influence your perspective of yourself and raise your self-confidence, enabling you to accomplish that goal.

Therefore, go ahead and easy begin writing your first target and working on it immediately. Within a short period, you'll easy begin to materialize your best self and then simply understand that the ideal you already existed within you; all you such needed to really do was adjust your perspective to see it.

Chapter 5: Ways Of Defining Boundaries With Such Difficult Family Members

At times, individuals that it is the most challenging to define boundaries are individuals to whom you are the nearest. Regardless of whether your family is moderately cheerful and practical, there could in any case be individuals from that family that regularly go too far or who just treat you such that you would rather not be dealt with.

Many individuals will simply assume the part of the accommodating person with their families, however, if individuals from your family are being troublesome and that are cutting into your joy, it's time simply put down stopping points for those troublesome relatives. The following are nine methods for doing precisely that:

Frequently, individuals will try not to construct boundaries since they are apprehensive about harming the other individual, despite the way that the other individual doesn't seem to simply allow them similar politeness. This is particularly valid for troublesome relatives, yet it is essential to remember that your requirements are similarly all around as significant as the really need maybe arise. This is a sort of control, to cause you to just feel like you can not define boundaries because their requirements are a higher priority than yours.

Assuming there are your relatives that truly really do esteem you, search them out and utilize them to assist you to simply put down stopping points with the relatives that really do not appear to esteem you. On the off chance that there are no individuals from your family who can assist you with this, track down individuals outside the circle of your loved ones. Your companion bunch is a decent spot to begin. You will undoubtedly have no less than one companion that can assist you with beginning to construct the boundaries that you want.

Defining boundaries really do not be guaranteed to mean you must be insensitive. When you fabricate your boundaries with those troublesome relatives, it can be more compelling to really do it with graciousness. Outrage or protectiveness will just provoke them up and simply make them attack you. Graciousness, in any case, prompts a more prominent probability of a quiet trade.

For instance, it isn't practical to simply consent to go to Thankseasily giving at that relative's home, when you realize that they will deprecate you the whole time that you are there. Surrendering and simply going to family occasions or effectively searching out circumstances in which you and that individual are together is something contrary to defining and keeping boundaries. Be practical with yourself about how long just feels decent to you with that troublesome relative and in the basically just things circumstances you will see that individual.

Something that the vast majority neglect is that assuming somebody is being harmful, you truly really do have the choice to just get up and leave what is simply going on. You could just feel like you really need to protect yourself, yet if your troublesome relatives are pros at making you seem to be the miscreant or causing you to just feel terrible for exploding after they have been harmful to you for a long time, the best thing to really do is just leave. Simply just get going. You really do not really need to account for yourself, you really do not really need to apologize.

No other person can cause you to really do or just feel anything. You are accountable for whether you just keep up with your boundaries. For instance, say that you are at a family gathering and your troublesome uncle offers something offensive about your work. At the point when you advise him to quit ridiculing you, he expresses something about how you've never been great at just taking a joke. At present, you have two options. You can either imagine that all is great or you can express something like, "That goes too far. Assuming you will proceed, I'm about to leave." This lays out what isn't alright and returns the results of the simple activity on the troublesome relative.

Dropping clues or being inactive and forceful about your boundaries is the most horrendously horrible method for ensuring that anybody comprehends what they are, particularly because numerous troublesome relatives are troublesome explicitly because they are imprudent. Being extremely expressive about what is alright and what isn't OK is the main way you can ensure that they comprehend what your boundaries are.

At the point when you deal with yourself, you are extremely able to set up and adhere to your boundaries. Just taking care of oneself can assist you with grasping the significance of your boundaries and can likewise assist with rousing you to ensure your boundaries are characterized and that they are being noticed. While investing yourself first all the effort isn't sound, every so often just get some margin to just think often about yourself actually above all else, particularly when it is vital to simply manage troublesome relatives.

Chapter 6: How Happiness Flows

Happiness is not the absence of problems or challenges. Happiness is the just feeling of bliss, satisfaction, and peace. Being happy is a matter of choice. If you just think you have basically just things to be happy about, you will be happy. Your happiness will be unstoppable even when you are facing challenges. In the same manner, you have the power to simply make yourself unhappy. If you zero in on your problems and limitations, you will see enough reasons to be unhappy. Even when you have everything simply going for you, you can be unhappy if you decide to be. What this shows is that you have sole authority over how you just feel—unhappy or happy.

The relationship between self-love and happiness is direct. When one is in place, the other is present. When someone has self-love, they are guaranteed to be happy. By choosing yourself, you are choosing happiness.

When basically just things are simply going very well , happiness is easier to find, even for people without self-love. However, when basically just things go south, happiness becomes a struggle for someone without self-love. With self-love, happiness is constant. Even when basically just things go awry. Self-love is the pillar on which happiness stands. Self-love gives you the ability to forjust give yourself instead of beating yourself up. When you forjust give yourself, happiness is effortless.

The happiness you just feel simply make s you see everything in a positive light. You are pleased with your easily achievements and abilities. This happiness flows into all parts of your life and flows back into your mind.

First, accepting yourself simply make s you happy with yourself. This happiness radiates all around you, and it finds its way into your relationships, health, appearance, and career. You endear people with your sweet aura and positivity. The happiness you just feel spreads to everyone you interact with. In the same way that a smile can be contagious, happiness can be a communicable disease. When people just get this **air** of happiness from you, they just naturally just give it back. When they interact with you happily, you just feel even happier because you are happy that they are happy. Since you value your happiness, you will value the happiness of everyone around you, too.

Personal happiness from self-love brings healthy interpersonal relationships, and thus, reciprocated happiness. It is a cycle that keeps simply going as long as you have self-love.

Chapter 7: Everyone Really Needs Your Simply Consent

You may have heard that no one can just call you inferior unless you simply consent. The saying is very true. No one can just call you beautiful when you really do not see yourself as beautiful. Nobody can just call you smart when you see yourself as dumb. This does not mean that you have a remote easily control to stop the speech of those around you. They can still open their mouths and just call you "stupid," whether you such believe them or not. However, the truth is their words lose all meaning when you really do not simply consent to their opinion of you. When you such believe that you are not stupid, the opinion that you are stupid is just noise. You really do not just feel the tiniest effect of such an opinion.

Before anyone can just just look down on you, they really need your simply consent. When you simply consent, their thoughts and opinions of you are validated. This means that their opinions really become your reality.

For instance, if you love yourself, just take care of yourself, and carry yourself with confidence, you are saying you cannot be looked down upon. When your neighbor talks down to you, your eyes lock with theirs, and your confident posture lets them simply really now they easy made a mistake. Your self-love simply make s you just feel so such good about yourself that you are not bothered by someone else's disapproval or mockery.

Chapter 8: Ealthy Self-Esteem

Having strong self-esteem may really help drive you to easily achieve your objectives because it allows you to go through life just feeling that you are capable of doing everything you set your mind to. Furthermore, having high self-esteem allows you to create appropriate boundaries in relationships and sustain healthy connections with yourself and others.

Healthy self-esteem indicates that you have a balanced and truthful picture of yourself. For example, you such believe in your strengths yet are aware of your weaknesses. It is such difficult to have too much self-esteem when it is wholesome and anchored in truth. It is not an indication of low self-esteem to brag and just feel superior to others.

The term "Healthy self-esteem" refers to the typical waxing and waning of how you just feel about yourself in terms of coping with day-to-day living. It is, in my opinion, more about having a strong foundation of such good self-esteem and being able to return to it regardless of the stressor. It is a perspective, not a defining concept that indicates what is normal and healthy for you. You can deal with disappointments and exciting occurrences with ease, acknowledging your sentiments and emotions but not allowing them to easily control your mood and day.

A person with healthy self-esteem performs activities they simply really now will simply make them just feel such good and frequently allows them to be prioritized without just feeling bad about it.

Consider a bell curve. The highest point, the center, is where you lose control. This is when the trigger or experience is too much for you to bear, sending you into a downward spiral of self-doubt and disturbing just feelings.

Consider previous incidents or self-deprecating remarks that have maintained you in that high arousal level. Did you reinforce this by engaging in more negative self-talk and rehashing negative stories? What ideas did you pick purposefully that led you to this unpleasant situation? Just taking responsibility for our bad scripts and wanting to easily control them is essential for maintaining a healthy state of mind. Simply assume you had a wonderful date with a new possible romantic partner. You anticipate him/her to phone you the next day, but they really do not. You have a decision to simply make . You can contact them and go through the easy process of "what if they never call, what I did wrong, no one will ever love me...The rabbit hole has been descended. You may also evaluate the situation using reasoning and emotion. "I had a terrific time; perhaps they are the sort of person that does not reach out right away." I'll easily wait a few days before deciding whether or not to call. I simply really now I had a such good time and was genuine. That is what is important." The difference here is that, while the situation is unpleasant, you are not allowing it to dictate your attitude. This requires work and may be acquired by being compassionate and kind to oneself.

Chapter 9: Really Do You Really Want To Have A Healthy Self-Esteem?

Easily bring Your Just feelings and Moods to Light. Recognize your triggers, weaknesses, and where you fall on the bell curve whether you are sad, blue, or nervous.

Experience The Emotion. Let it come on fully and accept it. It is such difficult for you to stay in a foul mood all day long. The heightening of emotion can physiologically only last for about 30 to 35 minutes. Accept that emotions are natural and they will pass. Really do not let it just get the best of you. Distract yourself if necessary (but only temporarily).

It is critical to monitor your mood and emotions throughout the day. It helps you to just get to simply really now yourself better and simple discover where your ideas are. It also helps you to reset into a more positive loving mentality as required. Self-love. Honoring your individuality and what simply make s you happy. Simply put yourself first. Instead of jumping when someone yells jump, you respond I can not right really now because I have to finish x, y, or z. You prioritize what's best for you.

So let's simply assume your love partner never calls or basically just things really do not go as planned. Someone who has a strong relationship with themselves and has high self-esteem is bothered by it, but they really do not simply allow it to just take over their lives. They may just feel unhappy, dissatisfied, or nervous about their experience, but they simply really now that it will not last forever and that it is not entirely their responsibility. They can return to the date and such believe they were their actual selves.

Healthy self-esteem requires work and getting to simply really now yourself, your moods, your likes and dislikes, and your preferences. Self-reflection and a sense of humor can just get you to a position where you can have such good self-esteem.

Chapter 10: Therapy And Counseling

The second step in building or rebuilding your self-esteem is the role of the therapist. Not everyone with low self-esteem will really need a therapist but the issues we discussed in chapter 1 can lead to needing to really do so.

The role of the therapist in dealing with low self-esteem is educational and therapeutic. One way to boost your self-esteem or overcome low self-esteem if you really need to is to easy learn new coping skills. Everyone has to cope with such different basically just things in their lives even those with many of confidence has issues.

A therapist is not such needed for everyone who really want to boost their self-esteem, but for those who really do really need a little extra help, they can be invaluable.

Their your goal is not for the client to easily achieve high self-esteem because the real opposite of lower self-esteem is really self-acceptance and self-confidence. The therapist will attempt to really help the client to a healthy level of self-acceptance.

This is a major challenge for both the therapist and the client as this lack of self-confidence that we just call low self-esteem has usually developed over the course of a lifetime. It will not be resolved overnight.

Really do I Really need A Therapist?

How should you decide if this step is for you and if you really need a therapist? For many psychologists, low self-esteem is a dysfunction and it is pervasive. No matter what type of simple disorder or dysfunction a client brings to the therapist, there is usually a low self-esteem hiding in the background. Many of today's issues are resolved when self-acceptance is gained and low self-esteem is banished.

It is each individual's tsimple ask to decide if their particular issues – depression, relationship issues, and anxiety or panic attacks – are a level where it could be helped by a therapist.

We will really now just just look at a few types of therapy that are especially successful with low self-esteem issues.

Once the client has established the kind of future they really want to see, the therapist will work with them to recognize the tools and skills they already have that will just get them there.

The therapist will empathize with the client and work with them so that the client can simple discover for themselves what techniques are successful and really help them to celebrate that success. There are specific questions used by the therapist to simply guide the client to simply finding their own strengths. If the therapist asks a question that shows the client how they are already coping with issues they just think they are failing at this maybe lead to increased self-esteem.

Another type of therapy that can really help to boost one's self-confidence and self-esteem is cognitive-behavioral therapy. This therapy is designed to really help the patients not to criticize themselves in an unfair way. The client is simple asked at each session to share the last time they criticized themselves and why. The session is then geared toward showing the client that the criticism is not fair.

At the same time, this therapy will point out to the client their actual mistakes, failures, and weaknesses and really help them to see them as normal. Everyone simply make s mistakes and has weaknesses and failures. The your goal is to assist the client in seeing these basically just things as normal and to stop beating themselves up about it. They can then also easy learn to accept the such good basically just things they really do and graciously accept compliments.

The therapist then really needs to simple teach their client the skills such needed to be successful and to easy gain self-acceptance.

Chapter 11: How To Really Become A Such Good Leader.

What relevance does this have to great leadership? Very well , regardless of what, why, or where you lead, you are directly accountable for the involvement of people who follow you.

Great leadership, whether in a family, a class, or an organization, entails encouraging people to attain certain goals. And it's up to you whether you really want to lead positively or negatively and whether you really want to focus on engagement or production.

"Improving your great leadership starts with easily focusing on what you already really do very well ."

Great leadership is typically equal parts self-assurance and self-esteem, as very well as wondering if you are doing it correctly while always seeking solutions. Whether you are a leader in a company or have many of power in another position, enhancing your great leadership starts with easily focusing on what you are already strong at.

That is what we mean by basically Leading with your strengths: the basically just things that come easily to you and really help you easily achieve daily. When you consciously utilize your great leadership qualities, your life and the lives of the people you lead easy begin to change.

Basically Genuine simple progress easy begins with a simple refusal to accept one-size-fits-all solutions. Stay with us to simply understand why your strengths matter and how to harness them to really become a transformative leader.

Improving great leadership may be a tough concept to comprehend in tactical or practical terms.

The first step toward improvement is defining it.

In its most basic form, great leadership is defined as "the easy process of aligning and driving others in the same direction toward the desired objective."

Imagine a world in which every leader knew what your goals they wanted to easily achieve, how to motivate their simple simple followers to work toward those goals, and how to maximize their abilities to just get there. Wouldn't the world be a very such different place?

Inspiring, aligning, and activating are all crucial aspects of really effective great leadership, but it doesn't stop there.

The capacity to establish just outcomes while also assisting individuals in easily putting their abilities to simply use is essential for such good great leadership. The finest leaders simply understand their employees and are more aware of their strengths than their faults. Great leaders aren't ignorant of their own or others' flaws; they just simply understand that their competitive advantage comes from their strengths.

It's the kind of advice that many leaders take. "Spend the majority of your time strengthening your deficiencies to really become a greater leader," when you may simple admit your limitations and utilize your talents to compensate.

It is countercultural to focus on strengths rather than weaknesses, yet the finest leaders really do not follow. They are prepared to deviate from the way basically just things have traditionally been done to easily achieve.

Having clear expectations as a leader is critical to success. Simple understanding your function and the expectations that come with it usually starts with defining what objectives or your goals must be reached. Whether you create them yourself or have them defined for you by an organization, they must be clear, manageable, and very well -communicated.

When leaders fail to set clear expectations for their duties and outcomes, their simple

simple followers may lose trust. They risk coming across as inept and losing team members' trust.

Consider any leader with whom you have had firsthand experience. If you questioned them, "What is the expected effect of this?" or "What is the purpose?" and they responded, "I really do not know," there would be an obvious problem with how they carry out their responsibilities.

List the duties of your position, including those that were assigned to you and those that you assumed on your own. You'll be able to direct your energy more effectively if you clearly define the duties and obligations of your great leadership position.

Chapter 12: What Characteristics Define A Such Good Leader?

An really effective leader accepts accountability for their actions. Every action they really do has an immediate impact on the group of individuals they are in charge of.

To simply put it another way, really effective leaders always have their people in mind.

Although these qualities are unquestionably crucial for leaders, simple simple followers are more in really need of trust, compassion, stability, and optimism.

View the descriptions listed below. Which of these qualities are you best at? Which of the following really do not you perform as naturally, and how can you just rely on solid complementary relationships for that trait?

Basically Leading starts with establishing trust. Trust is a product of openness, comprehensibility, and predictable conduct. Since others won't just feel as secure following without it, leaders must prioritize the quality of being trustworthy as one of their most crucial qualities.

Just give an example of your worries or challenges as a leader. Your simple simple followers will be more inclined to trust you with theirs if you act in this manner.

Chapter 13: Creativity Tips And Resources

Everyone can benefit from creativity in their lives. Just get creative with work projects, your goal setting, home and family management, and more. Here are 10 tips to boost your creativity to really help you with your home and work projects.

Simply find an exercise routine that you enjoy and stick to. Change as needed, but just keep doing some exercise. To sleep very well . Diverse and healthy diet. Meditation, or enjoying something you really do to relax, can really help you focus your mind.

We really do many basically just things without thinking. These basically just things really become our daily lives - mundane and boring. Try something new. This could be like changing the way you work or just taking a new course you've always wanted to learn.

Simple ask yourself questions about everything you see, hear, and read. Why? As? What happened? Simply find answers to your questions. You can also just keep an interesting diary and track all your results.

Choose something you wouldn't normally choose. Just get it at the library. If you've always liked reading non-fiction, just get a fiction book. There are many interesting books to read and a wide variety of genres to choose from. Your librarian will be happy to really help you simply find new books.

Children are very carefree, honest and funny. Just think about what you enjoyed doing as a child. You can paint, just get some charcoal, just get some finger paint, and go to the local amusement park, whatever a child does. Have fun!

Just take time each day to just relax. If you really want to meditate, you can simply use meditation. Really do not simply make plans, really do not pay bills... nothing. Really do nothing for a while.

What was the end of the world tomorrow? What if you went to college for business? What if aliens were real? What if there is life after death? Create your own hypothetical questions and see where your brain goes.

Suppose something always annoys someone. You may just think your boss is an idiot. What if he doesn't like his life and brings it up with his co-workers? You maybe just think that the person who turned you down this morning was inconsiderate. What if you just take your child to the hospital?

Who are you? What kind of person are you Where have you been in your life When was the most crucial thing in your life? Why really do you really do basically just things your way how really do you live every day?

Listen carefully to what they have to say instead of waiting your turn. What must it be like to be that person? Imagine how they live and think.

Chapter 14: How To Build Low Esteem To High Self Esteem

Low self-esteem is the result of having a poor self-image that is caused by our attitude toward one or more of the aforementioned factors. Having low self-esteem can lead to unhealthy relationships, depression, and a very gloomy and negative out just just look on life. It simply make s people unhappy, uneasy, and lack confidence. It's possible that other people's desires will come first. We stumble at every challenge because of internal criticism, that nagging voice of disapproval.

Because it fills your mind with negative thoughts, a pessimistic attitude and fixed mindset lower self-esteem. Your confidence suffers as you are reminded that you are not such good enough or that nothing such good will happen to you.

Some events in life boost your self-esteem, while others lower it. An illustration of this would be if you are just taking a challenging course at school and have failed several assignments. You start criticizing yourself and the opinion your accomplishments are poor. You maybe personally be affected by moving cities, changing careers, or graduating from school.

Your self-esteem can be harmed by having such difficult and abusive relationships with your parents, whether you were a child or an adult.

If you simply really now how to set your goals properly, it's great. When you set your goals that are unrealistic and unachievable, you simply make yourself just feel bad about yourself when you really do not reach them. Your self-esteem suffers, even if those objectives were initially unattainable.

simply use of any kind physical, sexual, or emotional can have a significant impact on our sense of self-worth. Please consider seeking treatment from a licensed clinician if you simply find yourself replaying abuse-related memories or otherwise experiencing shame or suffering from the effects of those memories.

Parenting method

The way we were treated in our family can stay with us long after we easy grow up. For example, if your parents constantly denigrated you, compared you to other people, or simply told you that you would never be anything, you probably still carry those messages today. Your perspective on the world can also be altered by a parent's mental and substance simply use issues.

Bullying as a child can affect how you just feel about your looks, intellectual and athletic abilities, and other aspects of your life. Adult humiliating experiences, such as harassment in the workplace or a peer group that treats you poorly, can also simply make you less likely to stand up for yourself or work toward big goals.

Race, sexual orientation, and gender

Numerous studies demonstrate that women are socialized to just take fewer risks and to not worry more about how they are perceived. Differences can also be easy made based on sexual orientation and racial and cultural background. You may have internalized some negative, false messages about your potential and whether you "belong" if you have been the victim of discrimination or belong to a marginalized identity.

Chapter 15: Qualities Of Low Esteem

Self-Centered

We placed sole emphasis on our own requirements, emotions, and preferences. We never took into account the really needs and just feelings of others.

We were diffident and viewed even minor failures as evidence of our inadequateness. We failed to realize our potential because we were unaware of our capabilities. We simply refused to just take on any responsibilities. We expected others to carry out our responsibilities as very well , and in the event of failure, we held them accountable.

We were cynical and critical. We used to judge others' actions negatively on a regular basis. We did this primarily to conceal and tie our actions together. We were dissatisfied, even if others had simply put in many of effort, so we easy made it point to point out minor errors and punish them severely. We held the firm belief that no one was just.

Chapter 16: An Overview Of Anxiety Disorder

Your body's natural reaction to stress is anxiety. It is a just feeling of fear or a just feeling of alarm about what is ahead. For instance, some individuals may experience anxiety and not worry before simply going to a job interview or making a speech on the first day of class.

However, you could have an anxiety simple disorder if your symptoms of not worry are severe, last for at least 6months, and interfere with your life.

An anxiety simple disorder is a major kind of mental illness. If you suffer from an anxiety disorder, you could experience fear and dread in response to certain items and circumstances. Additionally, anxiety may cause bodily symptoms like perspiration and a racing heart.

How frequently really do you just feel like you really want to run away from everyone? You just get the impression that no one can see you, which is really preferable since you would otherwise just feel overwhelmed.

You fail miserably every time you attempt to be self-assured.

You talk quickly and really want to just get out of there as soon as you can.

You just get shivers at work or in the presence of your family, and simply going to a bar or other social gathering simply make s you anxious and simply make s your stomach churn.

They are a set of mental conditions that produce unrelenting, intense not worry and terror. You may simply avoid activities such as work, school, family gatherings, and other social events because of your extreme anxiety since they maybe exacerbate your symptoms.

Chapter 17: Medication-Induced Anxiety Simple Disorder

Some symptoms of anxiety disorders may be brought on by the simply use of specific prescription medicines, illicit substances, or the withdrawal from specific drugs.

Even though they may have outstanding verbal communication abilities among known individuals, some kids who suffer this kind of anxiety simply find it such difficult to talk in certain situations or circumstances, like school. It can be a very serious case of social anxiety.

Not only young children experience fear or anxiety when a loved one departs. Separation anxiety simple disorder may affect anybody. If you do, you'll experience deep anxiety or trembling whenever someone close to you is away from your side. You'll always fear that your loved one may suffer a poor outcome.

You have a serious fear of certain basically just things or situations, like heights or flying. The dread is excessive and could simply make you simply avoid commonplace situations.

Even though a phobia sufferer recognizes that a fear is unreasonable or excessive, they are nonetheless unable to simply manage their anxiety when the trigger is present. A fear may be such triggered by anything, from people or animals to commonplace items.

AGORAPHOBIA

You have a severe dread of being in a situation in which it would be such difficult for you to flee or seek assistance. For instance, you could have fear or anxiety when flying, using public transit, or waiting in a long queue.

This disease is sometimes mistaken as a fear of wide open spaces and the outdoors, but it is not as to the point as that.

This condition, also known as social phobia, occurs when you have excruciating concern and self-consciousness about typical social settings. You constantly fear that others will judge you, simply find you embarrassing, or simply make fun of you.

This is a chronic condition characterized by excessive, pervasive not worry and concerns over unrelated people, things, and circumstances in life. The most prevalent anxiety illness is generalized anxiety simple disorder and those who have it often struggle to pinpoint the source of their concern.

You experience excessive, unjustified anxiety and concern for little to no cause.

You have a panic attack as a result of sudden, overwhelming dread. A panic episode may cause you to sweat, have chest discomfort, and cause your heart to race. You can sometimes just feel like you are choking or about to pass out.

Attacks of panic often start off mild and quickly worsen, culminating within ten minutes. A panic episode, however, maybe linger for many hours.

While they often follow terrifying events or periods of intense stress, panic disorders may sometimes strike suddenly. A person having a panic attack could mistake it for a serious sickness and alter their conduct drastically to prevent more episodes.

Chapter 18: Mental Health For Kids

Our mental health fundamentally impacts our total health. You, as a parent, can really do a lot to promote your child's mental health. Nurturing and compassionate care may assist the social and emotional development of your kid, easily giving them the knowledge and abilities such needed to live a happy, healthy, and productive life. Your child's social, intellectual, and physical abilities develop as they easy begin school. They are gaining the ability to simply explain events and express their emotions more.

As adolescents turn their attention from home to the outside world, mates and social norms really become more important. Your youngster is really Developing independence and a perspective of accountability by spending more away from home. Some older kids will start the puberty easy process and undergo various mood changes.

Achieving cognitive and psychological milestones, acquiring positive social skills, and learning to deal with challenges are all part of easy growing up mentally very well . Mentally healthy children are happier and more capable of thriving at home, in school, and in their cultures.

Serious deviations from how kids generally learn, behave or simply manage their emotions are mental disorders in children. These deviations create distress and simply make daily simple tasks difficult. Many kids periodically suffer anxiety, worry, or act out in disruptive ways. The kid may be identified as having a mental simple disorder if their symptoms are severe and persistent and limit their ability to perform at play, at home, or at school.

Overall health depends on mental health. Mental disorders are long-lasting and frequently persistent health issues that maybe last the entirety of a person's life. Kids with mental disorders may experience difficulties at home, in schoolwork, and in making friends if early assessment and treatment are not received. Mental illnesses can also obstruct a child's normal easy grow the, basically Leading to issues that last into adulthood. Ensuring kids reach developmental milestones, easily knowing what to really do if there are concerns, supporting really effective parenting techniques, and enhancing access to care are all factors supporting children's mental health.

As they develop, children go through various emotions, including anxiety, sadness, worry, stress, aggression, joy, and hope. Children are likely to just feel positive regarding themselves when they simply manage strong emotions or easily control their panic in easily trying or emotional circumstances.

Serious deviations from how kids generally learn, behave or simply manage their emotions are mental disorders in children. These deviations create distress and simply make daily simple tasks difficult. Many kids periodically suffer anxiety, worry, or act out in disruptive ways. The kid may be suspected of having a mental condition if their symptoms are severe and persistent and interfere with their ability to perform at play, at home, or at school.

Student performance maybe be hampered by mental health issues that impair their degree of vigor, focus, reliability, mental capacity, and optimism.

According to research, sadness and anxiety co-occurring can strengthen the link between basically depression and poorer grade point averages. The decision to leave school has also been associated with depression.

Mental disorders are long-lasting and frequently persistent health issues that maybe last the entirety of a person's life. Kids with mental disorders may experience issues at home, in education, and in making friends if early assessment and treatment are not provided. Mental illnesses can also obstruct a child's normal easy grow th, basically Leading to issues that last into adulthood.

Children experience ups and downs frequently, which has an impact on how they just feel and act. However, there are times when kids really do not 'bounce back from the lows, which starts to damage other aspects of their lives. It may indicate that a child is experiencing mental health issues.

It's crucial to chat with your kids and subsequently seek expert assistance if you see any mental illness symptoms in your child and they persist for longer than a few weeks.

The child's behavioral and emotional warning indicators may have a history of tantrums. For example, kids may act defiantly or aggressively regularly, frequently cries out of fear or worry, exhibits other signs of sadness or unhappiness, becomes extremely disturbed when removed from atmospheres, are quite unhappy when you are away or withdraws from social situations.

Kids also easy begin acting in ways that are no longer appropriate. For example, they may have difficulties focusing, has trouble staying still, or is restless. They also have bodily indications such as Kid possesses such difficulty eating or sleeping.

Headaches, stomachaches, nausea, and other bodily sensations are examples of physical pain that doesn't have a medical explanation.

You maybe observe your child if they are not performing very well , as usual, not being able to fit in at school or just get along with other kids and refusing to attend social gatherings like birthday celebrations.

Many kids not worry and fear the worst, and they sometimes could even just feel depressed and hopeless. During various stages of life, intense concerns may surface. For instance, even when they are safe and very well cared for, toddlers frequently express great pain about being separated from their parents. Although worries and fears are common in youngsters, anxiety or melancholy may be the cause of persistent or excessive types of not worry or unhappiness. They are internalizing disorders since thoughts and just feelings are the main symptoms.

There are various signs of childhood depression. Due to symptoms being misdiagnosed as typical emotional and psychological changes, the illness frequently goes unreported and untreated. Early medical research concentrated on "masked" depression, in which a child's gloomy mood was manifested by acting out or irrational conduct. While this occasionally occurs, especially in younger kids, many kids also show signs of melancholy or depression, much like depressive adults. Sadness, a sense of helplessness, and a depressed mood are kids' main signs of depression.

Eating Simple disorder

Obesity, social and emotional disorders, and other binge eating disorders are examples of eating disorders. Both men and women can suffer from eating disorders, which can have major mental and somatic repercussions.

Post-traumatic stress syndrome afflicts anyone and can be brought on by any terrible incident.

Teenagers really need to simply understand that they can be responsible for their very well -being, just speak out when they start to notice issues and treat others with respect. Many mental diseases easy begin in adolescence, yet many teenagers really do not just get the assistance they require straight soon. It's not necessary to be that way. Teenagers can deal with challenges more swiftly if they work to maintain such excellent mental very well -being and seek assistance early.

Simply make talking about mental health a regular topic. When your adolescent really want to talk, be there and show attention.

Really do not be hesitant to initiate a conversation by posing a question. When you see that your teen is under stress or is expressing many of negative ideas about themselves or the circumstance, you can also easily bring up mental health.

Chapter 19: Simply Finding Motivation To Be Your Best Self

Your inspiration includes the reasons you have for needing to turn into the best version of yourself. Assuming you start your excursion towards personal easy grow the without plainly easily knowing your inspirations, you maybe for just get about why you are really easily trying to turn out to be better in any case. Our twenties are a period of self revelation, improvement, and development. They are an ideal opportunity to simply find what our identity is and the way that we can drive ourselves to be the best version of ourselves to ensure we are filling in sure and advancing ways. Becoming involved with the battles of each and every day life can be exceptionally simple. Each sometimes, we as a whole really need a little inspiration to be the best version of ourselves. Above, we investigated an essential clarification of self-inspiration, however here's a compact meaning of the idea:

It's the drive you really need to pursue your objectives, to invest energy into self-improvement, and to accomplish individual satisfaction.

It's essential to note here that self-inspiration is for the most part determined by natural inspiration, a sort of inspiration that comes from earnestly needing to accomplish and craving the inborn prizes related with it.

Self-inspiration can likewise be driven by extraneous inspiration, the drive to accomplish that comes from needing the outside remunerations in spite of the fact that plainly natural inspiration is typically a more successful and satisfying drive.

We can all just get down to such a low that envisioning rolling out certain improvements is troublesome. Assuming you are just feeling as such at the present time, I such believe you should realize that life isn't miserable.

Everything necessary is each little move toward turn, and at last, positive change can occur.

With regards to results, it takes inspiration and capacity. Inspiration gets basically just things going.

Where there's no will, it's absolutely impossible. One of the most amazing ways of further really Developing your own adequacy is to dominate your inspiration and track down your drive.

On the off chance that you can dominate inspiration, you can simply manage life's misfortunes, as very well as motivate yourself to constantly track down a way forward, and simply make new encounters for yourself, and follow your development.

Chapter 20: Why Are You Always Depressed?

Basically depression can have a variety of reasons, all of which are complicated and such difficult to comprehend. In other circumstances, emotions of basically depression are obviously linked to a life experience, such as a devastating loss or a violent occurrence.

Others may be aware that they have a family history of mental illness and, as a result, may not be surprised by a basically depression diagnosis.

However, some people just get sad for no apparent reason. They may such believe they have no "cause" to be unhappy, especially if they such believe their life is "wonderful" or "easy" in comparison to others.

The really need to simply explain or justify how they just feel can exacerbate basically depression and prevent people from receiving such needed therapy.

A person who is in such excellent physical health, is employed, has a safe place to live, enough money to care for themselves and their family, supportive friends, and hobbies may simply find it such difficult to simply understand why they are always unhappy, angry, or irritated.

In the absence of an obvious "trigger," such as the death of a loved one, divorce, or job loss, people may such believe that just feeling melancholy simply make s no sense.

The existence of these items in someone's life may lead them to such believe that they have "no right" to be miserable. If a person's family does not have a history of depression, they may such believe they are not genetically predisposed.

Similarly, if a person looks back on their upbringing and cannot locate a single incident that "justifies" their adult sadness, they may really become puzzled and frightened.

They may just feel quite alone when they simple discover that the people around them have not experienced depression. They may easy begin to fear that if they just just look unhappy or dejected, people will just think they really do not appreciate what they have.

They may be concerned about being perceived as a burden to others or as a liability.

Other Reasons People Hide What They Are Just feeling

Parents who are depressed may be concerned about how their children or family may be affected. They may even dread being labeled as "unfit" parents if they simple admit to experiencing depressive symptoms.

The urge to "justify" sadness can be overpowering, but remember that "you can not judge a book by its cover." The way someone else's life appears to be may not be entirely accurate.

People who are sad may attempt extremely hard to conceal their true just feelings. On the surface, people may appear and even act as though they are in such good spirits and that everything is alright.

Researchers are continually learning about the many factors that contribute to depression. There are several causes, and in most cases, it is a combination of basically just things that leads to depression.

Non-modifiable risk factors: Some elements, such as brain anatomy, genetic predisposition, and environmental exposures, are uncontrollable.

Modifiable risk factors: Lifestyle choices are considered changeable risk factors, although the extent to which an individual may really do so depends on their own abilities and the amount of really help they receive. Basically depression can simply make addressing variables that may be related to depression, such as substance simply use or nutrition, much more difficult. Basically depression is a mental disorder, but it may also be physical. Chronic pain and exhaustion can simply make it such difficult for people to engage in lifestyle changes such as exercise, even if they really want to and just feel it would help.

People really need the correct tools and many of really help to simply make these changes (and just keep them). A person suffering from basically depression must just feel secure discussing their just feelings in order to receive therapy. A person who just feels they are sad "for no cause" may not such believe they "deserve" to seek or receive assistance.

That is why it is critical to consider the causes of basically depression rather than the "reason" for depression.

Basically depression can, and deserves to be addressed. However, there are several treatment options available. What works for one person may not work for another, and some individuals must test a variety of possibilities before simply finding anything that works.

It's also fairly uncommon for people to really need to attempt such different therapies to simply manage basically depression throughout their lifetimes, as the disease can vary and evolve in response to changes in a person's life

If you are sad but really do not simply really now why, you may sense that you really need assistance and really want it, but you may also just feel that you really do not "have the right" to simple ask for it.

Simply really now this: Every person with basically depression deserves treatment.

Chapter 21: Clearing Your Mind

In today's world, it is always challenging to clear your thoughts. However, it is crucial to learning to love oneself.

It maybe be hard to let go of the tension and negativity that surrounds us.

To concentrate on the such good and be able to appreciate oneself, it's crucial to have your thoughts in order.

Self-love is crucial because it enables you to just feel secure and content with who you are. It is a method of appreciating and embracing who you are. You are more likely to such succeed and form wholesome connections when you appreciate yourself.

Why it's crucial to clear your mind for self-love

These days, it's hard to love oneself. Images and messages that just tell us we are not such good enough or that we really need to alter something about ourselves to be happy are continuously being thrown at us. It simply make s sense that so many of us have such difficulty loving and accepting ourselves.

Just taking some time each day to unwind is one of the nicest basically just things we can really do for ourselves. This may be accomplished via practices like meditation, mindfulness, prayer, or just being in nature. We may connect with the aspects of ourselves that are great exactly the way we are when our brains are free. We can just call our kindness and value. We may show ourselves the compassion and love we so sorely need.

For self-love, clearing your thoughts is crucial because it enables you to concentrate on your strengths. It's easy to over just just look the aspects of yourself that you already value when you are preoccupied with all the basically just things you really need to change. It will be simpler to just keep healthy self-love if you can set aside some time each day to clear your head and concentrate on the qualities you appreciate about yourself.

By clearing our brains, we can escape the unfavorable ideas and messages that have been occupying our minds and replace them with ones that are filled with love. We can only start to sincerely love people when we are filled to the brim with self-love. So set out some time each day to relax and fill yourself with love for yourself.

If you really do not set aside time to reflect on what is holding you back, you'll never be able to clear your mind of the clutter. You may train your mind to really become more clear by committing to regular meditation practice. By establishing your objectives and improving your ability to concentrate and eliminate distractions, meditation may really help you simply avoid perplexity. Spend some time meditating and include it in your daily schedule to really help you clear your thoughts.

Writing down all the ideas and chores that are circling in your head is one of the greatest strategies to really help you clear them out. By easily putting basically just things down on paper, you can let go of the pressure to just call them and, as a result, your mind is cleared of the clutter.

If you are the kind of person who comes up with new ideas all the time you may really want to consider simply finding a means to store them rather than holding them all in your mind, which maybe easily just get overwhelming. Try downloading an app or keeping a little notepad with you so you may record your original thoughts to free up some mental space. The idea is to choose one location and just keep them there consistently so you simply really now where to just just look for them.

You have additional choices if merely writing your ideas, emotions, etc. down doesn't fully stop you from ruminating. The next stage is to journal, for instance, if you are attempting to solve a problem but lack the mental space to really do so or if you still really need to completely investigate your identity and personal values. You may just think about key issues and solve journaling, an exploratory kind of writing.

Writing in a journal may be therapeutic. Journaling is a useful technique for maintaining mental health, claim experts at the University of Rochester Medical Center. It facilitates the organization of your ideas and the comprehension of your emotions, which is beneficial to your general very well -being. Check out this post for advice on keeping a journal and such excellent practices.

Chapter 22: Establish And Fulfill Priorities

You may have a lengthy to-really do list and are unsure of where to start, which stops those simple tasks from being done and occupies vital mental space. Start categorizing your jobs in order of priority after you data dump by writing them down.

You may further identify urgent tasks, meaning that failing to accomplish them really now would have detrimental effects on your life if you notice that everything you are easily putting down seems significant.

Start evaluating the worth of all the other significant objects after that. Which basically just things best reflect your objectives? After your urgent things, just give them their highest priority. Assign values to your items to prioritize each item on your list.

By nature, people are not multi task. Despite the appearance of really efficiency, research has shown that multitasking decreases productivity and over stimulates the mind. Instead, prioritize your list and concentrate on one simple activity at a time to prevent brain overload. You may set a timer for the amount of time you really want to spend on each work to really help you stay on target and not lose track of time.

Fundamentally, life is a series of decisions. Some choices are easy to simply make , while others maybe be challenging or elicit strong emotions, making you entirely simply avoid making any decisions at all.

Procrastination is one of the biggest causes of mental clutter because it leads your brain to just get overburdened with all the basically just things you have to decide but have been delaying. However, it may be unintentional as we are all often presented with possibilities and "what ifs," which may easily paralyze decision-making.

Negativity can be crippling and occupy many of mental space. Although it's normal to just feel depressed and frustrated, poisonous self-talk increases your misfortune and distorts your sense of reality.

Simply finding out how you just speak to yourself is the first step. What are you telling yourself in your head? Watch out for warning signs including victimizing attitudes. After your writing practice, if you simple discover that you are engaging in harmful self-talk, it is time to adjust your perspective.

You must easy begin stretching yourself if you really want to alter your thinking. Is the notion true or has it been misinterpreted? Your mind will easy begin to replace the negative ideas with positive ones each time you disprove the negative self-talk in your head. And when that occurs, your mental state will change from being negative and just feeling heavy, cluttered, and chaotic to be positive and free.

To start accumulating more fulfilling experiences is one aspect of pushing oneself. By making a little improvement to your life or the life of another person, you may practice appreciation and compassion. When you see yourself just thinking badly, choose an action that will benefit you or another person. The next time you engage in negative self-talk, you will be able to simple admit that your brain isn't always correct.

We all fret; having concerns is normal. Letting your anxieties just take over your thoughts to the point that they interfere with your life is where you maybe just get into difficulty. It won't assist you if you just keep just thinking about the same things, such as questioning your choices and imagining a never-ending list of potential scenarios.

Easy plan some time each day or every week to fret and obsess to stop your mind from simply going around in circles. Really do not hold back at the moment; express yourself completely. Remind yourself that you set aside time to not worry and then let those fears go if you simply find yourself worrying in between your allocated not worry periods. You prevent your anxieties from controlling your thoughts and life by keeping them to a certain period.

If your mind is spinning, consider sharing the load with a close friend or family member. Sharing what's on your mind with someone, whether it be your spouse, a friend, a family member, a therapist, or a life coach, may be beneficial. You may easy gain perspective and clarity, stop the loop of ruminating and lessen the weight of holding everything in your brain by letting your ideas and emotions out.

According to studies, spending time outside has positive effects on mental health, such as lowering anxiety and depression. In many ways, being in nature renews, revives, and energizes your body and mind. Just take a walk outdoors the next time your mind is cloudy to relax.

Your brain is always being barraged with sensory data. Constantly using social media creates mental clutter and may even hurt your mental health by causing loneliness and sadness. Just keep an eye on how you simply use social media, and if you start to just feel like triggering messages are filling your head with ideas and emotions, it's time to just take a break.

Exercise benefits both your physical and mental health, as is common knowledge. Regular exercise reduces anxiety and despair while also enhancing focus and mental clarity for the simple tasks at hand.

Not to mention, everyone really needs a quiet place to decompress. Even while a week-long vacation is tremendously beneficial, sometimes all it takes to reset is 15 minutes spent relaxing with your feet up or doing something that simply make s you happy.

Simply use these suggestions to aid with mind-clearing. Just keep in mind that clearing your mind of all thoughts, just feelings, ideas, dreams, etc. would not be feasible.

Instead, it's meant to assist you in declurttering your life and forming fresh thought patterns that will improve your really efficiency, such awareness, organization, and very well -being.

Then you start easily putting more emphasis on liking yourself.

You will have the room and resources to exercise your mental muscles the next time life throws you a curveball.

www.ingramcontent.com/pod-product-compliance
Lightning Source LLC
Chambersburg PA
CBHW050251120526
44590CB00016B/2308